BRITAIN'S BEST KEPT SECRET

Ultra's Base at Bletchley Park

TED ENEVER

ALAN SUTTON PUBLISHING LIMITED

First published in the United Kingdom in 1994
Alan Sutton Publishing Ltd · Phoenix Mill · Far Thrupp · Stroud
Gloucestershire

First published in the United States of America in 1994
Alan Sutton Publishing Inc. · 83 Washington Street · Dover · NH 03820

Revised 2nd edition, 1994

British Library Cataloguing in Publication Data

A catalogue record for this book is available from the British Library.

ISBN 0-7509-0631-6

Library of Congress Cataloging in Publication Data applied for

Typeset in 12/13 Sabon.
Typesetting and origination by
Alan Sutton Publishing Limited.
Printed in Great Britain by
Redwood Books, Trowbridge, Wiltshire.

Contents

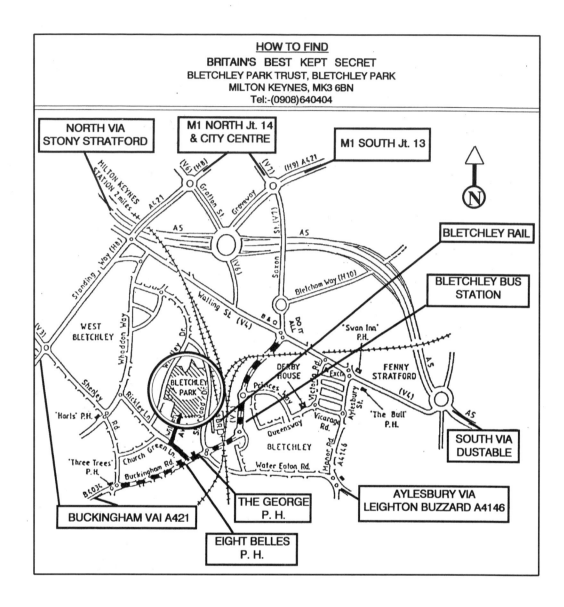

Foreword
by
Professor Sir Harry Hinsley

For more than a century now, Bletchley Park has had an important place in the life of the town and its neighbourhood.

Until the 1930s it was the residence of Sir Herbert Leon and his family. They served the interests of the community with the sense of duty that characterized leading families before the Second World War. Many people in the Bletchley area still remember them with gratitude and affection.

In 1938 the Mansion and its grounds were taken over as the wartime headquarters of the Government Code and Cypher School, known to the public now as the Government Communications Headquarters. This organization controlled all British cryptanalysis and carried out most of the work itself on the site of the Park and in other nearby country houses. It also transmitted the resulting intelligence, under the now famous Ultra code-name, to British, Anglo-American and United States operational headquarters in the United Kingdom, the Mediterranean and Europe. Such were its successes that the number of staff employed rose from under 200 in 1939 to nearly 7,000 by the middle of 1944.

So large a body of men and women, and one that was constantly entering and leaving the Park from the spring of 1940, when it began operating around the clock in three shifts, could not fail to have an impact on the life and thought, and the economy, of the neighbourhood. Billeted to begin with mainly in Bletchley itself, workers at the Park were eventually accommodated with families and in hotels and public houses in virtually every town and village within a twenty mile radius, Milton Keynes being one of the smallest villages in those days. At 8 a.m., 4 p.m. and midnight, and more frequently in emergencies, buses and station-wagons brought them in and took them home. By day, Bletchley railway station was thronged with people taking or returning from leave or a day-off in London. Cinemas and public houses were busy. Over and above their friendships with the families they lived with, those who worked at the Park were not cut off from their communities.

They never knew, however, what the local population thought about the nature of their work. They themselves were sworn to secrecy and, on the other hand, their tactful hosts refrained from asking awkward questions; if they had their suspicions, they did not air them. It was enough to know that Bletchley Park was engaged on war work.

The considerable physical reminder of that work – the Park and its huts and other buildings – have been used for a variety of purposes since the end of the Second World War. But they have remained sufficiently preserved for the Bletchley Park Trust to have been able to give them a new lease of life, taking them into the twenty-first century as both a national and local memorial to the important contribution that was made in them to the victory of the Allies.

Bletchley Park Trust Aims & Objectives

To secure for the nation the area known as Bletchley Park in recognition of the work of the Intelligence Forces carried out on the site between 1939–45, particularly in relation to the breaking of enemy codes. To develop on site museums of cryptology and the history of computing as Bletchley Park was the home of the world's first electronic computer in the 1940s and is recognised as the birthplace of the computer industry. To encourage any other museums development on the site, particularly if of a high-tech nature. To supervise and encourage commercial initiatives on site to assist the on-going funding of the museums complex as above, so long as these initiatives are compatible with the overall aims and objectives of the Trust.

The aims and objectives of the Bletchley Park Trust laid down on its foundation in February 1992.

1. The Park Under Threat

Walk through the big iron gates that mark the Wilton Avenue entrance to Bletchley Park and you find yourself in a time warp. The 55 acre complex, though in continual use since its famous codebreakers moved out when victory was secured in 1945, still retains the air of that bygone era. The Mansion, a large, Grade 2 listed Victorian house, continues its domination of the site, just as it has done for more than a hundred years, and sits like an architectural jewel in a sea of wooden huts and sprawling, heavily constructed brick and concrete blocks, most

The Mansion, Bletchley Park, where Commander Alastair Denniston brought the Government Code and Cypher School in 1938. Now a Grade 2 listed building, the Mansion is the only listed building on the 55 acre historical site. Denniston's office was the ground floor, bay-windowed room beneath the copper-domed roof on the left.

of single storey structure and exuding a permanence almost beyond belief. Now, fifty years on, Britain's best kept secret still looks, and feels, one imagines, much as it did during the wartime years, though now its wartime work is both better understood and valued and the site recognized as part of our national heritage.

But that recognition has been hard won and only came in 1993. As recently as 1992 there was a very real possibility that the owners, British Telecom and Government itself, would gain permission for redevelopment. Then, the bulldozers would have moved in and swept away the wartime buildings, so destroying for ever a vital piece of twentieth-century history and turning the site into just another housing estate. That has not happened, thanks to the efforts of the community based Bletchley Park Trust and the support it has received, not least from the Bletchley Park Club, the Bletchley Park Residents Association and most recently, since it has recognized and appreciated the historical significance of Bletchley Park, Milton Keynes Borough Council.

Throughout 1992 and 1993, my Bletchley Park Trust colleagues, Roger Bristow, Tony Sale, Peter Jarvis and I, gave guided tours of the Park to a wide variety of groups and individuals. These tours are still taking place and all of our visitors, of course, have a common interest – to learn more of the history of the site and particularly, the importance of the work carried out there during the Second World War. Much has been written already of the latter, especially by those whose personal involvement at the time can only now be understood fully by those of us of younger generations. So this narrative does not set out to tell the whole intricate story of the Park and its wartime role – indeed there is probably no one person alive today who could do that, given the organizational structure of the Park at the time, other than perhaps Professor Sir Harry Hinsley, who has been so kind as to write the Foreword. What it does hope to accomplish is to give the reader a brief insight into the place and the role of certain key 1940s buildings within the Park's sizeable complex, while at the same time relating anecdotes and tales which the Trust's own research has revealed. So, in effect, this book is the guided tour mentioned above, with its associated commentary.

Much of the information, however, has been difficult to obtain because of the impenetrable secret that has been Bletchley Park for the past fifty years. The Bletchley Park Trust has used its best endeavours to get it right, but this has not been easy, so bear with me please if some

A basic German army Enigma machine, one of some forty thousand Enigmas in use by Axis forces during the course of the Second World War. The board showing the electrical connections is at the front; the three rotor wheels of this model are hidden beneath their own cover between the locking bolts above the recessed alphabet.

aspects, known as they may be to individual readers, are perhaps slightly off-line. And if they are, and you can correct them, then the Trust would be grateful for this information.

With the Park's early priority the breaking of the German Enigma codes, it is worth looking at how the Allies first became aware of the Enigma machine and the German belief that its codes were unbreakable. The machine was invented as long ago as 1918 by an electrical engineer, Arthur Scherbus, who was born in Germany in 1878. In appearance it resembled an overgrown typewriter. By a series of rotor wheel settings and electrical connections, it could produce the most horrendous codes, all of them immediately changeable by resetting the rotor wheels and electrical connections. So, anyone not knowing these settings was faced with the problem of choosing between 150 million, million, million solutions. Easy to see why later, Germany's leaders believed the machine was infallible. Even in the unlikely event of a cypher being broken, adjusting the settings could immediately make that knowledge redundant by throwing up a whole new set of codes.

It was exhibited at the 1923 International Postal Union Congress in Germany where it was put forward as a machine for secure inter-bank communications, but it never took off commercially. In 1926 it was taken up by the German navy and when Hitler became Chancellor and Fuhrer in 1934, his Nazi Party was quick to exploit its military capabilities and significance. Polish code and cypher experts, already distrustful of the Third Reich, began to unpick Enigma's coding system with some success and invited French and British cryptographers to a secret meeting in the Pyre Forest, Poland, in July 1939, to update them on their findings. Before Germany invaded Poland just two months later in September, the hostile act which led to the outbreak of war, Polish cryptographers made sure that models of the Enigma machine were passed to the British and French intelligence services.

The British machine found its way to Bletchley Park via the Park's first director, Alastair Denniston, who had attended the Pyre Forest meeting and who began to build Bletchley Park as the hub of all wartime intelligence. After Churchill became Prime Minister he referred to the Park as his 'ultra secret' and so secret intelligence gathered by, and relayed on, by the Park's codebreakers was given the code name 'Ultra' from 1942 onwards. At any one time throughout the war, only a handful of top commanders were privileged to receive Ultra, and they were not allowed to divulge their source of information even to some of

Prime Minister Winston Churchill, Britain's wartime leader, who called Bletchley Park his 'ultra secret' and 'my golden goose that never cackles' in recognition of the mass of valuable information it produced with the minimum of fuss or ceremony.

their seconds-in-command. Now that this is known, it throws new light on the characteristics of certain wartime figures, not least perhaps Field Marshal Montgomery, who might well have disposed of Rommel and his Afrika Corps earlier in 1942 than he did. But more of that later, when the work emanating from various buildings is examined.

And what of the German High Command and their infallible machine? Throughout the duration of the war Hitler and his military leaders were totally unaware that at Bletchley Park most of their secrets were being read and the vital information passed on to Allied commanders in the field.

However, to return to the current status of Bletchley Park. There is no doubt that the wartime buildings are fortunate still to be standing, for the secrecy surrounding their wartime role, zealously guarded until thirty or more years after the war, has been, to some extent, their own worst enemy. That secrecy was vital during the war is self-evident. But for ensuing generations secrecy meant ignorance, and only at the eleventh hour has the public become aware of the Park's unique, worldwide influence on wartime activity and mounted the campaign that has finally brought international recognition for the site. Not for nothing, then, is Bletchley Park deemed 'Britain's best kept secret'.

The pattern of current events that led to the nation almost losing the Park began in 1986 when Milton Keynes Borough Council and Milton Keynes Development Corporation, the two planning authorities for the area, adopted jointly 'A Plan for Bletchley'. The plan was non-statutory but went through public participation and conformed with the Buckinghamshire County Structure Plan, its policy stating that: 'Bletchley Park be allocated as a "special study area" in which favourable consideration might be given to some high technology, science based, office/industrial development, training/educational, institutional and possibly some residential development, subject to the preparation of a Master Plan for the development of the area which has been approved by the two planning authorities.' It must be remembered, of course, that at this time neither of the two authorities mentioned was fully aware of the historical significance of the site.

The 1986 document went on to make it clear, though, that the two planning authorities would not permit material changes or significant intensification of development in Bletchley Park until a joint study had been carried out by them (Milton Keynes Borough Council and the

Bletchley Park today from the air. The Park boundary has been outlined on this photograph though the lake is easily seen, centre. The major H-shaped block top centre is 'D' block; Bletchley railway station is toward the bottom right.

The Park as seen from the cockpit of a Spitfire in March 1943. The now demolished 'F' block is clearly seen bottom right and the sprawl of buildings in the shape of a crescent just above the main Park complex are the former RAF and Army camps, situated in what is now the Rickley Lane and Whaddon Way/Whalley Drive residential areas of Bletchley.

Development Corporation) in concert with the County Highway Authority to 'ensure that a reasonable balance is achieved between the use of the land and the traffic generated'.

At this time there was a shift in political emphasis locally from job creation toward housing provision, which by 1989–90 was recognized policy. The wartime huts in the Park could conceivably have been useful for job creation, but not for housing. Nevertheless, to maintain the policy of 'mixed development' in the Park inherent in the 1986 plan, a 'commercial' component was included within the study which, if implemented, could have resulted in the re-use of some of the huts. Therefore, the only interest in retaining the wartime buildings was an economic one. As the study evolved the Borough Council's Planning Committee resolved in December 1989: 'That a Development Brief for Bletchley Park allowing a higher level of residential use of the site other than indicated in the adopted Bletchley Plan, be prepared for the consideration of the Committee.' Further to this resolution, the Committee on 10 January 1990 also considered the possible development of land known as 'the playing field' which abutted the Park on its extreme north-eastern boundary. The study was duly completed and surfaced in May 1990 as a Development Brief for Bletchley Park. However, the ideas put forward within the brief were not attractive to 'the market' and, by 1991, agents for the owners were proposing residential development for the site. At the same time the wider conservation issues at the Park were being revealed and the Borough Council, responsibly, took note.

The May 1990 brief therefore summed up the Council's development policies for the Park as an area ripe for the building of something in excess of 200 houses set within a miniature business park with open access to the public. During the next year Bletchley abounded with all sorts of rumours about the possible redevelopment and the local community began to voice its opinion about the impending change in character of the site and the demolition of 'our huts'.

By the early summer of 1991, the Bletchley Archaeological and Historical Society, fearful that the wartime history of the Park would be swept away by the developers, began to plan a reunion of those wartime staff members, both codebreakers and support personnel, with whom it had contact, which it would hold in October of that year. The object of the reunion was to document as much historical fact about the Park and its wartime operations as possible. The chosen date, Saturday 19 October, was the fiftieth anniversary of a letter sent direct by senior staff at the Park – Alan Turing, Gordon Welchman, Hugh Alexander and Stuart Milner-Barrie – to Prime Minister Churchill in 1941, calling upon him to give the codebreakers more resources. Churchill's response is now legendary. 'Action this day', he wrote on the letter before passing it to General Ismay, one of his aides, 'and report to me.' The codebreakers were quickly given their much needed resources.

That chilly October Saturday began my own involvement in the campaign to preserve the Park in the national interest. Former Milton Keynes Mayor, Councillor Roger Bristow, asked if I would address the codebreakers and give them some advice, as a media man, on how the plight of the Park could be brought to the interest of a wider public. He briefed me well, and by the end of our conversation we had agreed that a letter to the present Prime Minister, John Major, should go from the gathering, informing him of the Churchill letter of 1941 and calling for

The spartan conditions faced by cypher clerks at work in a Bletchley Park 'hut' during the war. Shift work went on around the clock in addition to the normal nine to five day shift.

FRIENDS of BLETCHLEY PARK
BLETCHLEY, MILTON KEYNES

The Rt. Hon. John Major P.C., M.P.
10, Downing Street,
London SW1.

Dear Prime Minister,

Bletchley Park

Fifty years ago we wrote to your predecessor, Mr Churchill, about Bletchley Park. We were engaged in deciphering the signals of the German and Japanese High Commands and in sending their messages to our own armed forces to help them in the prosecution of the war.

Mr Churchill believed our work to be so important that he ordered that all our needs should be met: the various authorities are agreed that our work contributed greatly to the successful outcome of the war.

Much of the work was - and still is - secret, so knowledge of the historic importance of Bletchley Park is perhaps not widely known. Navy, Army and Air Force museums are well known but a museum to commemorate the Intelligence Services which directed their aims has been sadly neglected.

Among the lasting effects of our work was the installation of the world's first electronic computer 'Colossus' in 1943: many of the computers now in use are descended from this original machine.

The name of Bletchley Park is of world-wide renown. The co-operation with our American allies was a model for subsequent collaboration.

A recommendation to list the original buildings as historic has been made by English Heritage and rejected by the Department of the Environment. We are at a loss to understand the refusal. Most of the site is as we left it in 1945 and we would therefore urge you to ensure that the place is preserved and put to a suitable use. The main loss has been the recent demolition, on the instructions of British Telecom, of the building which housed 'Colossus'. The buildings put up for listing are either in excellent order or can easily be restored.

We understand that there are well formed plans for a museum of cryptology and computer science to be established in Huts 3, 6 and 8, where we daily broke the key to the German 'Enigma' machine cypher. The mansion, lake and gardens, all well maintained, would make a first-class conference centre. There are many interested parties for these projects, if only the decision not to grant a preservation order is rescinded.

We would ask, Sir, for your help in securing our longer term aims as above and, initially, for any assistance you can give in securing a preservation order for the site.

We are, Sir,

Your obedient servants,

The letter drafted by the 19 October 1991 meeting of former codebreakers at Bletchley Park and delivered by the author to Downing Street. Among the signatories was Sir Stuart Milner-Barrie who, with others, had signed the Churchill letter fifty years earlier.

his personal support. Perhaps, most importantly, we agreed that public opinion might be mobilized by the formation of a charitable Trust.

I had not bargained on the resilience and guile of those wartime veterans. They listened attentively, then suggested that as a journalist, would it not be a good idea if I composed the letter for them? And could I do it now? There just happened to be a personal computer to hand. And as for the formation of a Trust, yes, splendid. But that would be better done locally, so could the young man – flattery will always win – go away and do something about it? The first tentative meeting was fixed before the afternoon was over; the PM's letter was composed, agreed and signed, with one of the signatories being the, now, Sir Stuart Milner-Barrie. I was able to deliver it by hand to Downing Street the following Monday morning while en route to a business meeting in London.

In early November Dr Peter Jarvis welcomed a few people to his Church Green Road home for that first meeting where a Trust steering committee was formed. As well as Peter and his wife Sue there was Roger Bristow, Tony Sale, a senior curator at the Science Museum and secretary of the Computer Conservation Society, Ena Halmos, the then chairperson of the Archaeological and Historical Society, Peter Wescombe, who had the original idea of the reunion and had done much of the organizing of the 19 October meeting, and myself. Sue Jarvis volunteered to keep the minutes and the meeting asked me to become chairman, with Roger Bristow as vice-chairman. Using various good offices and part of the planning budget of Milton Keynes Development Corporation, who asked us as a consultant group to produce a historical brief and video on the Park, the Bletchley Park Trust, though not airborne, was certainly on the runway.

For the reader, it is time at this point to start the guided tour and the commentary, beginning with the long history of ownership of the site and the influence on the Park and on Bletchley itself of a much loved family. The formation of the Trust, and a short review of the activities which have ultimately saved the Park, is dealt with in Chapter 11.

2. The Mansion and the Leons

After the Romans left Britain about AD 400, various settlements grew in the region we now know as North Buckinghamshire. Among these was a clearing within an area later to be known as Whaddon Chase and made by a man named Blecca. It is from Blecca that Bletchley gets its name, 'ley' being a clearing or grassed land. So, over the centuries, 'Blecca's ley' has become 'Bletchley.'

Part of Etone Manor in medieval times, the first reference to Bletchley as a separate manor is found in 1499. Prior to this we know that the estate, to use contemporary wording, was given by William the Conqueror to one of his notable commanders at the Battle of Hastings, Bishop Geoffrey, of Constance, in Normandy. The estate was subsequently won and lost by several families. A certain Walter Gifford was made Lord of the Manor in 1092 by the then king, William Rufus, but died childless. His principal relative, Richard de Clare, took over and called himself the Earl of Buckingham, which apparently seemed not to annoy Richard the Lionheart who, in 1189, formally gave the manor, or estate, to de Clare. In 1211 de Clare's daughter married Sir John de Grey and the manor passed into this family line, de Grey becoming Baron Grey de Wilton, from where the current entrance to Bletchley Park, Wilton Avenue, gets its name. At this time records show that the present Bletchley Park was the deer park of Sir John's estate and in 1563 mention is made of a moated keeper's lodge in the middle of this deer park. The manor was to remain in the hands of the Wilton family until 1614.

In 1616, after the Crown had confiscated the de Grey lands following charges of treason against Lord Thomas Grey, who died in prison, the estate was given to Sir George Villiers who was created Earl of Buckingham and later, in 1623, Duke of Buckingham. He was followed by the second Duke, also George, but in 1674 he sold the estate to Dr Thomas Willis, a famous physician in the reign of Charles II. Following

Sir Herbert Leon, perhaps Bletchley's greatest benefactor.

the death of Dr Willis in 1699, the estate passed to his son, Dr Browne Willis, whose wife, by coincidence, was a direct descendant of Walter Gifford, the Lord of the Manor in 1092.

It was Browne Willis who, in 1711, first built a substantial house on the site of the present Mansion in Bletchley Park, which he named Water Hall, but by 1798 the house and adjoining lands had been sold and the house pulled down by the new owner, Thomas Harrison, a steward to the Northampton Spencers, the family of Diana, the present Princess of Wales. In the late 1870s, a descendant of the Harrison family sold the estate to a Mr Coleman who built the first part of the present day Mansion. By 1881 the property had come into the ownership of Samuel Seckham who enlarged the building before selling it on, a year or so later, to Herbert Samuel Leon, one of Bletchley's greatest benefactors.

Herbert (Sammy) Leon was born on 11 February 1850, the second son of a Jewish financier and founder of the stock exchange firm of Leon Brothers, which Sammy entered at the age of twenty-four, rising to become its senior partner. Just before he entered the firm he married, but sadly lost his wife, Esther Beddington, after only two years, leaving him with two small children, a son, George and daughter, Kitty. Some years later, in 1880, he was to marry again, his bride being Fanny Hyam. The marriage was to last for forty-six years, until his sudden death in 1926.

An ardent Liberal, Sammy Leon was a long standing friend of Lloyd George, who was a frequent visitor to the Mansion, the family's new home at Bletchley Park. In 1891 Sammy Leon became Liberal Member of Parliament for North Bucks, a seat he held for four years before losing it to the Tory candidate, Sir Walter Carlisle. He was destined never to return to Parliament again but his loyalties to the Liberal Party did not go unrewarded and in 1911 he was made a baronet. Immediately, he dropped the name Sammy and became known as Sir Herbert Leon, but change elsewhere was not noticeable, particularly locally. He continued to support Bletchley in many ways, and the current Leon recreation ground, the building of Leon Avenue, the Leon cottages in Church Green Road and many other property projects remain as evidence of his largesse. One of the town's current major comprehensive schools is also named after him. He was a good employer who rewarded loyalty and every Christmas a bullock from the estate was slaughtered and the meat distributed to his estate staff.

Sir Herbert's initials and date over the main entrance to the Mansion. He greatly extended the house during his lifetime and its new front was the final phase, much completed as shown in 1883.

However, you can't please all of the people all of the time, as my own market-trader father used to say, and Sir Herbert did not find favour with members of the suffragette movement, who chained themselves to the Park's main gates, or with the nearby rector of St Mary's church, Revd William Bennitt. Sir Herbert hated the sound of the bells, apparently, which he could not help but hear, the Mansion being only yards from St Mary's. Many times he tried to stop the bells being rung but the rector stuck to his guns, pointing out that the church had been there for 700 years before Sir Herbert came to Bletchley. Only as Sir Herbert lay on his deathbed in 1926 did Revd Bennitt grant his request. But once the funeral had been held, the bells pealed out again from St Mary's ancient tower.

Sir Herbert was sorely missed. He had established Bletchley Park and its grand house, the Mansion, and nearby Home Farm – now the

The proximity of the Mansion to those dreaded bells! St Mary's tower seen through the Park's current back gates. The house is less than 100 yards from the church.

site of Home Close, a small cul-de-sac of residential houses off Whalley Drive – as a thriving estate. He was good at making money via the North American stock market, breeding cattle, which he exported to South America to help build up the Argentine herds, and his orchid houses in the kitchen gardens of the Park were a joy to behold. But life had to go on and for the next ten years his wife, Lady Fanny Leon, continued his good works, not least by allowing the Park to be used for the annual Bletchley Park Show, which was the town's major event during the years between the two wars and for another score or more years following victory in 1945. Lady Fanny died in January 1937 and on her death the *Bletchley District Gazette* reported: 'Lady Leon can, without dispute, be described as Bletchley's greatest benefactress. Her generosity towards and interest in many of the town's organisations are well known. What will never be fully known are those many acts of kindness which have so endeared her to the people of Bletchley.'

During the Leons' lifetime at Bletchley the Mansion was enlarged considerably. From the small house purchased by Sir Herbert in the nineteenth century, the 1937 building had grown in size to the building that now takes pride of place in the Park today. As soon as he acquired the property, Sir Herbert added a domestic and servant wing. In this wing is the ice-house, used for cold storage of meats and produce and which, from the outside, is often mistaken for either a large, brick built dove-cote because of its shaped roof, or a private chapel, owing to its stained glass windows. After 1883 Sir Herbert extended the property by further stages, taking it forward and adding the drawing room, dining room and main entrance hall and lounge hall that can be seen today. The lounge hall has a stunning glass painted roof.

Architecturally, some will argue that the Mansion is a hotch-potch of styles, but to those of us living locally, it is a constant reminder of

The south side of the Mansion in the late 1800s. The pathway, lawn and flower beds were to become the site of Harry Hinsley's Hut 4.

The Mansion's ice-house in late 1993, with its lower windows boarded up after British Telecom vacated the site. The upper windows are those of stained glass.

The Mansion's library with its large ornate fireplace.

The exquisite ceiling and opulence of the ballroom, one of the largest rooms within the Mansion.

Sir Herbert and is a magnificent country house, boasting huge fireplaces, ornate ceilings and panelling.

By the time of Lady Fanny's death in 1937, storm clouds were already gathering in Europe as Nazi Germany steadily grew in power and influence. Sir Herbert's son George, the second Baronet, had made his own life and was ready to dispose of the Bletchley Park estate which was split into various lots and duly sold off. The Bletchley Park that we know today, bounded by the older Church Green Road and the newer Whalley Drive and Sherwood Drive, was one such lot, as was Home Farm and its surrounding land, running adjacent to the main London to northwest railway line.

The buyer of the Bletchley Park parcel was a local consortium of developers headed by Captain Hubert Faulkner. A keen horseman, Captain Faulkner would often appear on site dressed in riding or hunting wear and his plan was to break up the Park into smaller parcels of land

The panelled dining room of the Mansion, used as the Officers' Mess during the war years.

for residential development. He intended to demolish the Mansion and build himself a new property slightly to the south, on the flat ground used as a croquet lawn by the Leons alongside the lake. He began his site clearance in the stable yard, and took down some stables at the eastern end which were flanked to the south by the Leons' apple, pear and plum store, a building which was destined to make its own impact on twentieth-century history.

That, however, was as far as any substantial demolition plans were destined to go, for in the next year, 1938, Captain Faulkner was approached by Government agents representing a branch of the Foreign Office, the Government Code and Cypher School (GC&CS). The School, it appeared, was looking for a quiet country

The sale of Bletchley Park in 1937 as advertised by Knight, Frank and Rutley following the death of Lady Fanny Leon.

retreat from which to carry on its Foreign Office duties – though Captain Faulkner was not, of course, told what those duties were! The deal resolved was that the School would lease Bletchley Park for a three month trial period and then let Captain Faulkner know the position. The School quietly moved in, went about its business for the three months and then went away as discreetly as it had arrived. But, very quickly, it was back on the scene, and though I confess to having no official documentation on the sale of the site to GC&CS, it is perhaps correct to assume that this was a compulsory purchase whereby Captain Faulkner and his consortium had little say in the matter.

By the late summer of 1938 the School was established at Bletchley Park under Alastair Denniston and had begun its radio eavesdropping and codebreaking tasks. A special radio room, high in the roof of the

Mansion under a turreted tower, was quickly constructed by partitioning off part of the stop-cock room under the tower, the tower itself housing two large water tanks, one of marble, one of slate. The radio room, small and cramped, was given the codename 'Station X'. The radio's aerial was slung between the finials of the Mansion's Victorian roofline before running to a tall cedar tree some 30 yards or so from, and almost in a direct line with, the main entrance at the front of the building. Here, the Royal Navy riggers who carried out the work secured the aerial to the tree with a base plate before taking it on at roughly a 45 degree angle to an elm tree standing close to the lake. From this tree the aerial passed through two more elms which stood roughly in line with where the edge of the present tennis court stands, diverting later to Hut 1, before turning at 90 degrees to complete the loop on the Mansion roof.

As warclouds continued to gather, despite Chamberlain's Munich dash and the 'piece of paper' newsreels from Croydon airport indicating a peaceful coexistence with Nazi Germany, GC&CS at Bletchley were quick to realize that should war come, German radio tracking devices could easily pinpoint Bletchley as a listening source. And Bletchley, even in these earliest of Government establishment days, was already being groomed for its codebreaking role, a role that was to be kept totally secret not just from the enemy, but from the British themselves for many, many years to come.

The result of this policy thinking was that Station X, and the aerials spanning the trees and roof, were quickly dismantled and a new base established some seven miles to the south-west at Whaddon Hall. At the top of the big cedar tree at the front of the Mansion the Navy riggers left the base plate still firmly attached to the trunk. Over the next forty years the tree grew round the plate, so giving it a somewhat unique two-pronged top. In the gales that swept the country in October 1987, one of the prongs snapped off, leaving the tree today with its single, kinked top.

But if Bletchley Park had no direct radio links, how was it to receive the coded Enigma messages being sent by wireless transmission by the enemy? The answer was the 'Y' stations, a series of listening posts around Britain who sent the messages to Bletchley either via motor-cycle dispatch rider or by direct teleprinter line. As the war went on, more listening stations came on stream, though among the most notable and original were Chicksands Priory, near Shefford, Bedfordshire, Chatham and Flowerdown, in Wiltshire, and Scarborough, Yorkshire. Meantime,

The Park's famous Station X radio room was housed in the Mansion's turreted water tower, viewed here from the Victorian tradesman's entrance.

The cedar tree at the front of the Mansion, used by Royal Naval riggers as an initial anchor-point for aerials in 1938 and damaged by gales in the 1980s.

the Mansion, or more generally 'BP' as the site began to be known in Government circles, began to build up its number of personnel under the guiding hand of Alastair Denniston. Described as a small, bird-like man with very blue eyes but of great intellect, Denniston was billeted at the home of Sir Everard Duncombe at the Manor House in Great Brickhill. As a young teenager, Philip Duncombe remembers Denniston, and two other BP companions also billeted with his parents, exchanging nothing more than meaningful glances when the BBC radio news relayed particular items concerning the war. Philip – now Sir Philip, the vice-chairman of the Bletchley Park Trust and who still lives at the family home at Great Brickhill – realizes now that Denniston and his colleagues knew what the BBC would be reporting long before the events became public.

Denniston's office in the Mansion was the bay-fronted room to the left of the main entrance and during 1938 and 1939 he spent considerable time interviewing bright young mathematicians completing their education at Oxford and Cambridge. This gives a distinct pointer to one of the three reasons why Government chose Bletchley Park as its main intelligence gathering base, for Bletchley is exactly halfway between the two varsity cities. The other reasons were its strategic location, for the main London to northwest railway line is only yards away, and one of the nation's major trunk roads, the A5 Watling Street, a mile away across the fields. The telecommunications cables and wiring, going direct into London, followed the line of the Watling Street, so making direct, but secret, contact easy.

3. The Sentry Box and the Bombing of Hut 4

After standing in front of the Mansion and contemplating the individual styles of its various parts, brought together to form the whole rather like vertical slices of a gigantic cake, the visitor has access to both sides of the building. Go to the left and you are immediately confronted by Hut 4, one of the early wooden huts constructed in 1939 and painted green. Hut 4, about 145 feet in length and some 30 feet wide, is complemented by a small extension at its end nearest the rear entrance to the Park.

The naval Enigma hut, Hut 4, as it is today, the home of the Bletchley Park Club.

The interior of Hut 4 as it never was in the 1940s. Current members of the Bletchley Park Club enjoy a 1990s drink on hallowed ground; the 1941 Battle of the Atlantic was won from here.

The hut was used mainly for naval codebreaking and it was here that the Enigma code book, captured from U-boat 110 on 8 May 1941, was duly delivered. This had the greatest impact on helping to break the German naval codes, of course, and led directly to the Allies winning the first Battle of the Atlantic. Following this victory, Commander Hans Meckel, a German signals officer at the time, was sent by his commander, Admiral Doenitz, to question whether Enigma was foolproof. Interviewed by Bletchley Park Trust researchers in Berlin in 1992, Commander Meckel reported: 'On more than one occasion I was sent to ask about Enigma and each time I was told, "Don't worry; it is completely safe."' Hut 4 also handled information on other naval campaigns such as the Mediterranean. It was also the hut where a young academic, Harry Hinsley, later to become Professor Sir Harry Hinsley, Master of St John's College and Professor of the History of

International Relations at Cambridge, pitted his wits against the talented adversary. . . .

Part of the fascination of the Bletchley Park story is how its own secret was never broken and the extraordinary lengths that its misinformation sections went to in safeguarding its existence. An instance that may well have been part of Hut 4 work at the time of the Mediterranean and North African campaigns of 1941 and 1942 was when Field Marshal Irwin Rommel, desperate for supplies from Italy, became dismayed when a series of naval convoys were systematically picked off by British submarines and aircraft. Only food was getting

Hut 4 brought a young Harry Hinsley into prominence. By 1944 he was aide to the then Director of the Park, Sir Edward Travis, and they are pictured here on a visit to Central Bureau, Melbourne, Australia, in that year. Sir Harry is second left, wearing a bow tie; Sir Edward is third from the right. Within the group are high ranking US, Australian and British service personnel and the Governor of Queensland, Sir Leslie Wilson.

One of only two remaining sets of Second World War garage doors remaining on site, these are behind the Mansion at the entrance to the stable block.

through; arms, ammunition and troopships were being sunk. Enigma decrypts at Bletchley were showing the exact compositions of the convoys and therefore only the food ships were allowed through, strategic policy indicating that there would soon be many German and Italian prisoners to feed in North Africa. To cover any possible thoughts Rommel and the German High Command might have that Enigma was being broken, Bletchley sent out its own signal, in a code it knew the Germans were breaking, which congratulated a mythical agent in Lisbon on his convoy intelligence and awarded him a substantial pay rise!

If the visitor should choose to take the small road that runs on the right hand side of the building, then this leads past the ice-house and, turning left, to the rear of the Mansion. Turn to the right, and you pass under the clock tower entrance to the stable block. Before making any turn, however, the visitor is confronted by a set of garages which still boast their wartime corrugated iron doors, strengthened by appropriate iron crosspieces. Let's suppose, though, that the turn is to the left. Just to the left again is a small courtyard that houses the rear entrance to the Mansion. It is from this vantage point that the best view of Station X is afforded, the turreted tower seeming totally out of place amongst the more visually acceptable pitch of the Victorian roof. A stone slab set in the wall by the old position of the Mansion rear door is clearly inscribed 'Tradesman's bell' and immediately evokes memories of the grand house and its servant staff. The bell that would have once hung by the slab and which the tradesmen callers would have rung to have gained admittance is no longer there, but close by remain buildings that formed an essential part of everyday life for Sir Herbert and Lady Fanny Leon.

These are the two landau houses, where the family carriages were kept and which form one side of the courtyard. Though one of the pair

The stone block showing the position of the tradesman's bell at the back door of the Mansion.

has been forced to accept a modern door and some infilling, the Victorian woodwork and window on a gable end are still in good condition. More Victorian-style woodwork is repeated just across the courtyard in the roofline of what was Sir Herbert's Rolls-Royce garage and workshops. In its heyday the garage was lined with beautiful pine panelling but some years ago part of this was ripped out and the eventual fate of the wood unknown. Much, though, still remains. When GC&CS acquired the Park in 1938, VIP vehicles were initially housed here but, as traffic flows increased, the vehicles were moved elsewhere and the building used for general purposes.

Towards the far end of the garage wall, fronting this rear entrance roadway, is the remains of an old gate post built of brick and stone. On the other side of the road sits its mate, in slightly better condition. These were the two posts which marked the original site of the Mansion rear

The wartime sentry box at the back gates, built tight up against the old kitchen garden wall and to where dispatch riders would first report before delivering their vital 'Y' station messages. An original door to the garden remains, as can be seen.

gates in Sir Herbert's time, but early in the war the gates were taken down and moved several yards further back toward the church, so creating the rear entrance and gates on view today.

Immediately inside these gates is a wartime sentry box, built of brick with a concrete roof and slit, glassless windows, the brickwork beginning now to show the ravages of fifty years of rain and frost. In the early days of GC&CS operations in the Park, only VIPs were allowed to use the Wilton Avenue entrance and all other traffic had to enter the site by this gate, itself accessed by Back Lane, a turning off Church Green Road now signposted 'St Mary's Church – parking!' However, as staffing numbers in the Park grew, and because the flow of traffic became so great, this entrance was unable to cope and the main gate came into general service once more. Throughout the war though, the back gate entrance was used by dispatch riders bringing the coded Enigma signals from the 'Y' stations. There are reports that at peak times of activity, up to forty riders an hour would converge on Back Lane from the various listening stations scattered across Britain. A busy time for the sentry on duty.

Opposite the sentry box, on the Mansion side of the entrance, is a small wooded copse, mainly of firs and believed to have been planted by Sir Herbert, possibly in the hope of deadening the sound of the bells from the church tower only yards away.

On the night of 20 November 1940, a lone German bomber crossed Bletchley. Either having become separated from the main attacking squadron heading for the Midlands, or on a tip-and-run, target of opportunity mission, the bomber is thought to have been trying to pinpoint and attack Wolverton Works, some four miles north of Bletchley. At the time, and until quite recently, the works was a major railways carriage and wagon construction and repair yard. During the same era Bletchley station was served by its own loco sheds and goods yard and was an important junction in its own right, carrying the Oxford to Cambridge branch line across the main London–northwest tracks. From the air, on a murky night, Bletchley station might well have been mistaken for Wolverton Works.

The six bombs dropped by the lone raider fell some 400 yards off target. The first landed in Rickley Lane, now a properly constructed road but in those days little more than a track across the fields. The second badly damaged or demolished the stables and laboratory wing of Elmers School, another local imposing Victorian residence used for some codebreaking and training purposes by GC&CS though demolished some years ago. Its grounds are now the site of Elmers Park, a residential development of twenty-four detached houses. The third bomb plunged into the copse close by the sentry box and went deep into the soft earth bank, held by a retaining wall of York stone.

The soft earth enveloped the blast which, rippling through the ground as a shock wave, moved the extension to Hut 4 several inches off its 'sleeper' brick foundations. The fourth landed in another earth bank beyond the Mansion's stable block but did not explode, and the fifth and sixth landed harmlessly in open fields towards Home Farm, possibly on what was later to be the site of the Park's massively constructed 'F' block and annexe. The bomb that did not go off was unearthed by demolition experts next day and the fuse and explosive removed safely; maintenance men jacked up the extension to Hut 4 and literally pushed it back into place, reportedly without interrupting the important naval codebreaking work going on inside at the time. Whether there is any truth in a Wren rating working there at the time writing home to say that she had now experienced the earth moving is another matter!

The spot just inside the back gates to the Park where the bomb dropped in 1941, the blast moving Hut 4 off its foundations.

4. The Stable Block

Turning around at the back gates and retracing steps along the road, past the rear courtyard of the Mansion and the wartime garages, the eye is met by the ornate Victorian archway-cum-gatehouse which is the entrance to the stable block and yard. Here, time literally does stand still, for the large clock, in the centre of the arch and put in place by Sir Herbert's builders all those years ago, has not moved its hands for a very long time.

The yard is enclosed on three sides, its only open end being to the east where Captain Faulkner knocked down a total of eight horse boxes after purchase in 1937. The drains in the floors of the boxes are still visible. Three linked cottages, all of various design, make up the north side of the yard and were used as estate dwellings in Sir Herbert's time and for staff accommodation during the war. Cottage 1 was the Victorian head groom's house. Later a Mr Sanders lived here and he was head gardener and pig keeper – even during the war the Park produced its own bacon. Cottage 2 was Sir Herbert's old feed and granary store. The ground floor was later turned into a flat and the lead-

The wartime pigeon loft with Commander Denniston's garage beneath. The extended brickwork is clearly visible.

The time warp that is Bletchley Park – the clock at the entrance to the stable yard permanently registering fourteen minutes past four!

lined feed bins in the roof dismantled. A roof light was let into the tiles and the old stairs replaced. There is a small turret on the front of the building which houses the new stairs. Cottage 3 was the original tack room serving the stables. This also became a flat, then was enlarged into a full-sized dwelling which became the home of the site's cafeteria manager.

On the west side of the yard is a row of stables which were turned into garages during the war. The middle one of these sits under the estate pigeon loft and was extended by some two feet in length around 1939 to accommodate Alastair Denniston's Rover car, the newer brickwork clearly visible. There are no reports of the car needing to be cleaned more than any other so we can surmise that the flooring of the loft was sound! The Trust does have a record of the amount of feed purchased for the pigeons during the war, and has made contact with

Sir Herbert Leon's apple, pear and plum store on a snowy morning in February 1994. This was the building used as the 'think-tank' by Alan Turing and others to develop the world's first computer.

the sons of the two pigeon keepers at that time. Many of the pigeons went regularly to Thurleigh, an American airbase in neighbouring Bedfordshire, from where they were transported into occupied France before bringing back messages to the Park.

It is perhaps the buildings on the south-west side of the yard, however, that had the most significant wartime role. This is Sir Herbert's apple, pear and plum store, to which earlier reference was made. A long low building, it was originally two stores but knocked into one to form a bungalow prior to GC&CS coming on site in 1938. It was in this building that the earliest recruits of note to Bletchley Park were sent to 'study' at the outbreak of war. It became the Park's famous 'Bungalow' or 'Cottage' over the years, a 'think-tank' building with varying groups of mathematicians and what were later called 'boffins' meeting and working in its various rooms. There is some evidence that very secret work was carried out here during the latter part of 1939 and throughout 1940, though certainly Alan Turing

One of the few pictures ever taken of the highly secret Colossus with its Wren operators. Mark 1 was powered by 1,500 valves, the Mark 2 by 2,500 valves.

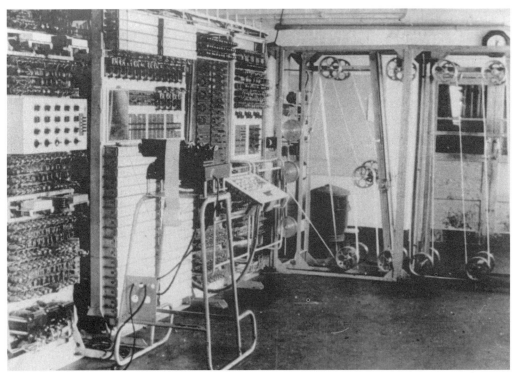

More detail of Colossus showing its circuitry and pulley-wheel system.

worked here a little later on what we now know was computer research, possible splitting this with other codebreaking duties that he carried out in Hut 8.

Turing was joined in his computer research in the building by other top mathematicians on the Park. Also playing a leading role was Dr Tommy Flowers, from the General Post Office research station at Dollis Hill, who argued, and won the day, that the thermal valve should be used as switching gear. Between them they devised the 'Heath Robinson' machine, as they called it, a mass of cogs, wheels and pulleys supplementing the advanced electronics which they hoped would break high-grade German codes more rapidly. The 'Heath Robinson' machine worked and became the forerunner of the world's first electronic, programmable computer, 'Colossus', which was assembled in the Park in December 1943 and was playing a full part in codebreaking activity by the time of the D-Day landings in June 1944.

Colossus stood some 16 feet long, was about 12 feet deep in places, and about 8 feet high. It was a formidable piece of equipment and has accorded Bletchley Park the honour of being the birthplace of the computer-led society in which we live today. This in itself had to remain a secret for thirty years, until 1975, so when, in the 1950s, North American mathematicians and scientists 'invented' the computer, it could not be refuted. Colossus ran on some 1,500 valves but this early model, Mark 1, was quickly followed by Mark 2, which was even more powerful and operated on 2,500 valves. As the world of electronics has evolved, transistors replaced valves, only themselves to be overtaken by the microchip. A modern microchip the size of a thumb is now capable of performing the tasks undertaken by Colossus fifty years ago.

By the end of the war, ten Colossus machines were operating in Bletchley Park and the methods used in some of their calculations are still deemed secret. We may never know fully what work these early computers carried out; perhaps one day it may be revealed in Cabinet papers via the Public Records Office. What we do know is that the machines worked on codes from elsewhere than Germany and Japan, but significantly were used to break high-grade codes coming from more advanced German encyphering machines, including those used by Adolf Hitler himself and a few other top ranking Nazis. These machines included the 'Geheimschreiber' or 'secret writer' and the Lorenz. So successful was Colossus in this operation that towards the end of the war, had mobile phones as we know them today been invented, it would have been quicker for Goering and Himmler to have telephoned the Park to obtain the Fuhrer's orders rather than to wait for them to be decoded at the German end!

At the end of the war all ten Colossus machines on site were broken up for security reasons. However, in concert with the Computer Conservation Society, the Bletchley Park Trust is already forging ahead with a rebuild to go on show in the Park, the building team headed by Tony Sale, who has been given the utmost cooperation from GCHQ at Cheltenham. The wartime Colossus machines were operated by highly trained Wren personnel who, of course, never said a word to anyone about the work on which they were engaged.

There is one final point of interest regarding the stable yard, and that rests literally at the visitors' feet. The modern tarmac surface sits on top of a large underground, vaulted roofed, water storage tank some 70 feet in length. With Sir Herbert making his Victorian estate self-supporting,

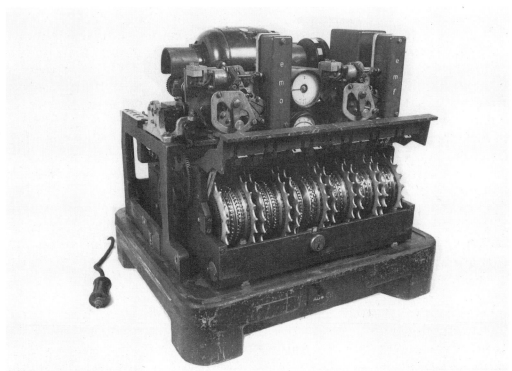

The highly-technical and complicated German Lorenz machine, its codes produced via a 12-rotor system but broken by Colossus. The Lorenz went on public display for the first time at the Bletchley Park Trust's open weekend and exhibition in the Park on 26–27 February 1994.

the Park had its own electricity supply. The current was produced by machines which, at times, needed cooling and water was drawn from this underground reservoir for the purpose. The reservoir was believed to be fed by run-off water from the kitchen garden and when full, decanted its overspill via a channel into the lake some 100 yards away.

5. The Wooden Huts

As I have already mentioned, almost every building in Bletchley Park is termed 'a hut', no matter how big or strongly constructed it may be. But the original huts are true to the name, being constructed of Canadian pine and the outside covering being either shiplap boarding or asbestos sheets. The remnants of the collection of initial wooden huts that

Almost as well photographed as the Mansion – Bletchley Park's famous wooden huts where the first codebreaking teams, other than those in the Mansion, were formed. The building in the foreground, numbered 53, is Hut 1, the birthplace of GCHQ, Cheltenham. The centre gable end belongs to Hut 6, responsible for all early German Army and Luftwaffe codes, while the darker hut in the background is Hut 3, the priority hut. The lowered and crumbling bomb-blast walls run alongside Hut 1 and Hut 6.

remain today – Huts 1, 3, 4, 6 and 8 – are probably the most photographed buildings on the site after the Mansion.

Built in the earliest days of GC&CS occupation of Bletchley Park, the huts were transported in sectional form from Guildford. With Captain Faulkner still on hand, GC&CS gave him the task of overseeing their building and the huts were quickly assembled on low brick 'sleeper' walls. Local carpenters – including many undertakers who, in those days, made their own coffins so were skilled woodworkers – were detailed to report to the Park, with Sunday included as a working day. Bob Watson, who worked in the Park and its outstations for almost forty-five years as a carpenter and joiner, was one of this team. He still lives locally and in his contribution to the recently published book *Codebreakers*, edited by Sir Harry Hinsley and Alan Stripp, he reports that the huts took shape as if they were coming off an automated assembly line.

Bob's family have been associated with the estate for many years – his grandfather was the carpenter who constructed the wooden framework which supports the large copper dome on the Mansion – and Bob was there when Hut 1 became operational. A small building only 40 feet by 16 feet, Hut 1 was linked in to Station X via the aerials erected by the Royal Navy riggers and as such is accredited with being the birthplace of GCHQ, Cheltenham. Mention was made earlier of Whaddon Hall taking the Station X role and when, after the war, Whaddon Hall was decommissioned, the electronic surveillance moved to Hanslope Park, close to the Northamptonshire border. Hanslope become known as the Diplomatic Wireless Service and though Hut 1 in the Park is unused at the time of writing, Hanslope Park is still a thriving Government establishment.

But it was Huts 3, 6 and 8 that were to emerge in history as the key codebreaking huts. And, as their importance grew, so did their staffing needs, so that by the end of the war Hut 3 was no longer a single wooden 1939 structure, but a whole range of locations and buildings on the Park. The same can be said for the other huts and that caused some confusion at the 19 October 1991 reunion. Local researchers would proudly show a former Luftwaffe codebreaker the wooden Hut 6, for example, with a strident, 'Well, here it is; you're old workplace!' only to be brought down to earth with an equally forceful: 'Sorry. I never worked here. I worked in Hut 6, you see, a big concrete building . . .'

Part of the wooden hut complex viewed from the corner of Hut 3, with the crumbled bomb-blast wall of Hut 6 now almost non-existent.

The somewhat scruffy appearance of some of the wooden huts is not merely due to the ravages of time. Their coverings were at some time in the past treated with an intense preservative that repels paint, so no matter what is done to the outside woodwork or surface, it continues to look decidedly second-hand. Hut 3, on the other hand, carries its age a little better, being faced with asbestos panels now painted earth-brown. The hut, owned by British Telecom, carries the name Spencer House, perhaps after the Spencer who once owned the site all those years ago.

Hut 1 has been mentioned already and Hut 2, sited close to a fir tree on what is now the Mansion car park, was demolished in 1946. Believed to have been used as a communal hut, reports also abound that this was the NAAFI hut where tea and buns were dispensed to service personnel and codebreakers alike. Hut 3, however, is considered by many historians to be *the* hut, certainly as far as the early days of the war are concerned.

As can be seen from site plans, Huts 1, 3, 6 and 8 enjoy a close geographical proximity. Huts 1, 6 and 3, in that order walking from the Mansion, were protected in the war years by a bomb-blast wall that was built about two feet away from only some of the outside walls of the buildings. The wall was about nine inches thick and was as high as the eaves of the building. Little of this wall remains now, except one section around Hut 3, but from this one can imagine how difficult was the job of fastening and unfastening the blast-proof shutters that covered the windows, when whoever did this job had to squeeze into the two feet gap. None of these shutters remain today but they were hinged at the bottom with a clip latch fitting. They covered the entire window and when opened rested on the back of the bomb-blast wall, so somewhat restricting natural light. The wall only ran around some exterior parts of the huts, for the huts themselves were considered to be protecting each other in places, because of the way in which they were sited.

So to Hut 3, for it was here where some of the earliest decrypting took place and where the sorting and prioritizing of messages was carried out. All the major events during nearly six years of conflict were known about by the teams of staff working from Hut 3, whether in its original location or, as it grew, from all its other locations throughout various buildings on the Park. In many cases, strategic decisions were directly affected by information and advice proffered by Hut 3.

The original building itself is roughly an equal L-shape, its asbestos cladding shielded by a pitched roof covered in weatherproof felt. It is one of the few, if not the only, hut constructed to be totally independent if the need should have arisen. It has its own boilerhouse and central heating system, the only hut to be accorded this comfort, and the old pipework is still in place today. One leg of the 'L' was used as general offices, the other boasted somewhat larger rooms, one about 30 feet square being the area where information gained from the decrypts was prioritized and then sent to Whaddon Hall for transmission. Another room of about the same size is thought to be an original transmission room before Whaddon Hall took over, for wartime teleprinter cabling still remains on its outside walls.

As the importance of Hut 3 grew, so it was decided it needed extra protection and the roof was reinforced with anti-shrapnel sheets. But this meant additional weight, of course, and so additional bearers, in the form of metal poles, had to be used to prop up the metal sheeting. One of these 'new' reinforcement poles is still in the building today.

The role of Hut 4 and its important naval codes work was outlined in Chapter 3. However, Hut 4 worked closely with Hut 8, one of the longer of the wooden huts, being 155 feet long and 30 feet wide. Like Hut 3, it is asbestos covered and was used for the attempted breaking of German naval codes, an area where Alan Turing was eventually successful with codes produced by the updated, four-rotor Enigma machine, so winning for the Allies the second Battle of the Atlantic in 1943.

At the end of Hut 8, nearest the Mansion, is a small covered area where bicycles can be parked, much in use during the war when this form of transport was used by nearly everyone. Alan Turing was no exception and regularly cycled from his lodgings in nearby Shenley village. However, the chain of his bike was prone to come off every so

Hut 8, the second naval Enigma hut, sited behind Hut 1 and Hut 6. The open-fronted cycle shed at the end was a parking spot much favoured by Alan Turing. The stepped entrance shown is a secondary entrance; the main entrance faced the side wall of Hut 6.

often and Turing's mathematical mind calculated that it jumped off every fourteen revolutions. So every thirteen turns he would make sure it was firmly in place . . . A sufferer from hay-fever, he often wore his gas-mask on his journey to work, on more than one occasion causing the local population to think the enemy had attacked with poisonous gas.

Finally, Hut 6, already famous via Gordon Welchman's book *The Hut 6 Story*. Used for decrypting both German army and air force codes in the early stages of conflict, its importance can be gauged by its geographical location immediately alongside the key hut, Hut 3. Hut 6 unquestionably dealt with all the major campaigns and codebreaking operations of the war and was possibly the busiest hut of all, dealing as it did with two sections of the German military machine. Luftwaffe codes gave much of the early work and from Hut 6 Air Chief Marshal 'Stuffy' Dowding was alerted to Goering's Battle of Britain plans and was able to deploy 'the Few' accordingly.

Dowding has never been accorded, in my humble opinion, the recognition given perhaps to other senior commanders. But this is perhaps an instance where the secrecy of Bletchley Park throws new light on why that recognition has not been forthcoming.

Dowding was accused by some of his senior staff, notably Leigh-Mallory, of being overcautious in sending up Spitfires and Hurricanes in 'penny numbers' to take on the hordes of enemy aircraft sent by Goering to bomb Britain into submission. Leigh-Mallory wanted his boss to employ the 'big-wing theory', everything up in the air at once. What Leigh-Mallory did not know was that Dowding's information, via Bletchley Park, was that this was exactly what Goering wanted: lure all the British aircraft up at once so that by sheer weight of numbers they were overpowered.

Dowding, then, refused to be drawn, and sent up small pockets of planes to get in among the massive German squadrons to cause as much confusion as possible. But he could not tell Leigh-Mallory *why* he was following this strategy, and could not even use his privileged information to defend his own rank and position when, later during the war, he appeared to be passed over.

Breaking the Luftwaffe codes proved to be easier than breaking the naval codes. In those early wartime days the German Luftwaffe were somewhat arrogant, for victory against Poland, the Low Countries and France had come easily. England was bound to follow the same pattern.

This underestimation made the Luftwaffe slack in its own internal discipline, particularly where Enigma was concerned. The code book gave precise instructions on when rotor settings needed to be changed, but the Luftwaffe often ignored the code book. After all, Enigma was unbreakable, wasn't it? The result was that Bletchley was given more time to concentrate on the current codes being used and they were duly broken.

The German Navy, on the other hand, were sticklers for correctness and followed the code book rules to the letter. Breaking these codes, therefore, was the much harder proposition.

The rear end of Hut 6 and the front end of Hut 3 are only a few feet apart – so close, in fact, that to speed up the passing of information from one to another, a small wooden connecting tunnel was built at about shoulder height. Bob Watson built it and tells how high technology of the day was used to tell 'next door' when material was on

Bob Watson points to the spot on Hut 6 where more than fifty years ago he cut the opening for the connecting tunnel with Hut 3.

the way. A Wren banged the inside of the tunnel with a broom handle! The material to be passed through was loaded into a sliding wooden tray fitted with a cup hook at either end to which string was attached. After being alerted by 'next door' it was a simple matter to pull the tray through using the string or to use the broom handle to give the tray a healthy shove. Not only did the tunnel genuinely save time, it also protected precious 'perms and sets' hairdressing from being ruined when it was pouring with rain because the Wrens no longer had to run between huts with the relevant documents. At the end of the tunnel's useful life in 1945 it was dismantled, but where it sat can still be seen quite clearly.

On the Army front it is very probable that a Hut 6 team – either in this original building or from an expanded location – dealt with the campaign to push Rommel's Afrika Corps back from the threat to Egypt and the Suez Canal in 1942. It was this campaign and the use of Bletchley's intelligence that perhaps better outlines the character of Field Marshal Montgomery. Far from the public image of the go-get-'em commander, the Park's secrets now reveal that he was extremely cautious and initially, anyway, did not put great store by the information given him by the Bletchley codebreakers.

When first told of Bletchley and its Ultra role, Montgomery insisted he should be the only military commander to be given the information. When this was denied by Churchill he treated the information somewhat sceptically and, on more than one occasion, refused to attack Rommel's divisions in North Africa when Bletchley knew them to be extremely weak, claiming that he wanted to build his own reserves even further to be absolutely sure of victory. This led to some heated exchanges with the Prime Minister and the same extremely cautious approach was to show itself again, two years later, in Normandy.

Opposite this collection of huts are two tennis courts, built on the site of what was Sir Herbert Leon's maze. When Prime Minister Churchill visited Bletchley Park in 1940 he stood in Alastair Denniston's office in the Mansion and watched staff playing rounders on the old croquet lawn by the lake. When he asked Denniston what recreational facilities were on the site he was told there were none. At that time the remnants of the Victorian maze were being pulled out to make way for a new car park but Churchill would have none of it. 'Tennis courts, Commander,' he is alleged to have told Denniston. Today, Bletchley Park still boasts the only tennis courts in Britain built by Prime Ministerial command.

The tennis courts opposite the wooden huts, built by Prime Ministerial command.

This visit was Churchill's only official visit to the site of his beloved Ultra, which he referred to as: 'My golden goose that never cackles' and its Wrens as 'hens that laid eggs without cackling'. Certainly it, and they, gave him many golden eggs, and all in silent secrecy, and on this visit he gave a brilliant impromptu speech to the assembled staff. But he is believed to have visited on other occasions, coming into the Park direct from Bletchley station via a special entrance. At the back of the engine sheds of the day, the local Home Guard patrolled outside what they were told was a special air-raid shelter. Though they guarded the entrance, they were never allowed in. All the evidence points to this being a tunnelled entrance to the southern end of the Park, through which VIPs – and these included Montgomery and Eisenhower – entered the site direct from trains pulling in to Bletchley. Certainly in the undergrowth which now fronts the present station car park wall, there are the remains of very large concrete pipes, or channels, which may have formed such a tunnel. The bulk of this, however, was probably destroyed with the building of a new road to serve the railway station, Sherwood Drive, after the war.

6. The Bombe Unit

Just across the small road from Hut 3, flanked by Churchill's tennis courts and its own back-up electrical generator building, is Hut 11A, known as 'the bombe unit'. No, it is not a place where they made bombs, for this bombe carries an 'e' at the end and was the name given to an electro-mechanical machine which helped in the breaking of the coded messages brought in from the 'Y' stations. The bombe unit itself

A side view of Hut 11 – the bombe unit room. Note the thickness of the reinforced roof as Bletchley Park entered its first phase of concrete, steel and brick building.

was something over 6 feet high and 6 feet-plus wide and was devised in its earliest form by Polish codebreakers at the outbreak of war. Its workings were refined by the British and it proved to be the mechanical bridge between manual codebreaking and the computer age, which began with Colossus in late 1943.

Though unassuming from the outside, Hut 11A is massively constructed, for the machines needed to be given as much protection as possible so that their vital work would not stop, even during a possible sustained air attack. The walls are 2 feet thick and are topped with an interlocking roof of concrete slabs. These are cemented together, with a further concrete covering overall. The support beams for the roof are 18 inch steel girders embedded in concrete, which are themselves supported by 12 inch steel girders, also embedded. This roof complex is held up from floor level by 15 inch

The front of the bombe unit with bicycle parking ever important! A unit went through the inner doors, just visible within the entrance now marked '18', with only inches to spare.

The current interior of the bombe unit. Since the war skylights have been introduced as well as some partitioning. The main steel girders of the building's frame are now boxed in.

steel girders, embedded in the concrete floor of the building, which has a ceiling height of only 8 feet.

The walls contain more steel girders at 2 feet intervals and within, and interlocking the walls, is chicken wire. A brick skin gives the outside face. Immediately below the ceiling line were eight small escape windows, only 18 inches square, and some of these remain today. They let in very little light and did little in the way of providing ventilation, so that when the machines were running – which was almost continuously – the room became very hot indeed. Small wonder that the Wren operators dubbed the bombe unit 'the hell hole'. The double doors at the southern end of the building give a fair indication of the size of an individual unit, for they were specially constructed for such access. Throughout the war the units were continually upgraded and five different types of bombes were ultimately in use. However, these in Bletchley Park were the very first to come on stream and it was in this

Visitors to the Bletchley Park Trust's first open day early in February 1994 examined some of the original fuses used to carry current to the bombe unit in Hut 11.

building that the first Enigma codes were broken mechanically, from 1 August 1940.

A mains electric cable enters the building at ceiling height in one corner, presumably so that the integral strength of the building is unaffected. The fuses used in the main fuse boxes are registered as 900 volts by 60 amps and the smaller fuses, used it is thought to run the units themselves, are 600 volts by 30 amps. Clearly, the machines needed a great deal of power and hence the generation of so much heat. The main feed of electricity for the whole of the Park came from two massive generators sited behind Hut 3 but in the event of failure the bombe unit had its own back-up supply as mentioned. This building was also heavily constructed and has a very substantial concrete roof. As the war progressed and the Park's workload increased, additional bombe units were sited at many locations throughout North Bucks, including Wavendon House, Adstock Manor, Gayhurst House,

A bombe unit room similar to that at Bletchley Park in Hut 11. This is probably at Stanmore, Middlesex, the giveaway being that Hut 11 did not have such a high ceiling.

Whaddon Hall, and a farm at Drayton Parslow. Units were also believed to be at nearby Woburn Abbey, in Bedfordshire, and were certainly at Stanmore and Eastcote. By 1944 there were at least two hundred individual machines in use at these various locations.

To the rear of the Park's bombe unit building is a much larger hut, Hut 11B, which was built in 1941. Though not so heavily constructed as the bombe unit itself, which pre-dated it by a year at least, it is still substantial and was used to train the Wren operators. Lessons were obviously learned from 'the hell hole' for Hut 11B boasted a large air conditioning unit to make life more pleasant. Quieter times post-1945 are indicated outside the building, for on one wall sits a small lean-to greenhouse, used by one of the Park's gardeners after the war.

7. The Homes of Colossus

Walking on from the bombe unit, and ever further from the Mansion, visitors will see on the right and to the rear of Hut 3 the two buildings that housed the main engines producing the electrical power for the Park – one large exhaust still rears itself from one roof. On the left is a small open space, with loose chippings on its surface, which in turn runs into the largest grassed open area in the Park. This grassed area was once the home of many of the ten Colossus computers that operated in Bletchley Park.

The grassed open space that was once 'F' block and its annexe, the main home of the Park's ten Colossus machines. The main frame of Colossus number one stood in the foreground of the picture, the site of the annexe.

The York stone paving that marked the top of Sir Herbert Leon's ha-ha wall is still clearly visible at the edge of the annexe site.

Where grass and chippings meet is a short line of flat York stone slabs. The slabs are all that remains of the top of Sir Herbert Leon's ha-ha wall which ran right across the Park, separating the domestic and ornamental gardens from the adjacent farmland. Keen gardeners will know all about ha-ha walls, particularly if their penchant is for formal Victorian design. But for those less interested in horticultural pursuits, I will try and explain as best as a layman can.

A ha-ha is a ditch about 10 feet or more deep, cut straight down on one side with the other side sloping gently to normal ground level. In effect, it is a dry moat and meant that Sir Herbert could stand on top of the straight side – topped with the York stones – and look out and past the sloping side to admire the prize cattle which earned valuable export orders. The gentle slope meant that the cattle could not be injured if they wandered that way, but the straight side gave an effective barrier. Fond of his cattle as he was, there was a difference between fondness and having them trample all over the lawns, hence the ha-ha which was as effective as a hedge or fence, but allowed the additional benefit of an uninterrupted view.

An impression of the Tunny machines in Testery looking from the doorway into the engineers' workshop. The door at the far end leads into the filter room ~ the only authorised way into the Tunny room.
Loose furniture, fluorescent lights and blackout curtains have not been shown.
From memory with help from Frank Crofts and Gil Hayward.

Ken Hatton
16-1-94

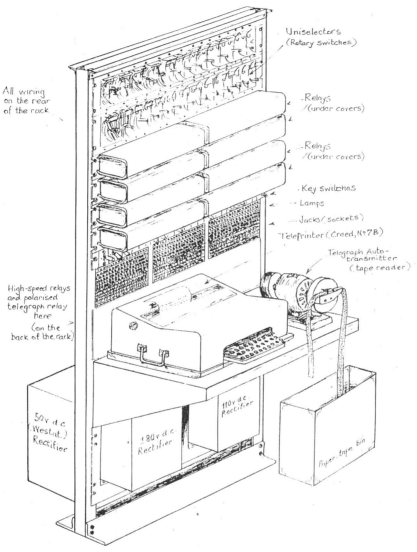

Uniselectors
(Rotary switches)

All wiring
on the rear
of the rack

Relays
(under covers)

Relays
(under covers)

Key switches

Lamps

Jacks (sockets)

Teleprinter (Creed, No 7B)

Telegraph Auto-
transmitter
(tape reader)

High-speed relays
and polarised
telegraph relay
here
(on the
back of the rack)

50v d.c.
(Westat.)
Rectifier

180 v d.c.
Rectifier

110 v d.c.
Rectifier

Paper-tape bin

TUNNY RACK

Front view

As remembered by
Gil Hayward
Frank Crofts and
Ken Halton

Ken Halton
16-1-94

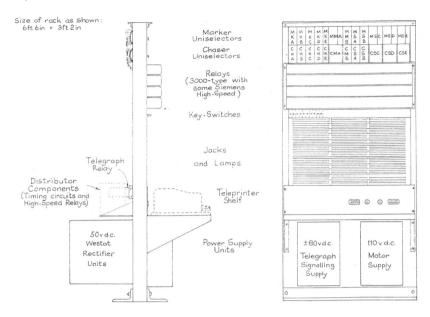

Size of rack as shown:
6ft 6in × 3ft 2in

Marker
Uniselectors

Chaser
Uniselectors

Relays
(3000-type with
some Siemens
High-Speed)

Key-Switches

Jacks
and Lamps

Telegraph
Relay

Distributor
Components
(Timing circuits and
High-Speed Relays)

Teleprinter
Shelf

50v d.c.
Westat
Rectifier
Units

Power Supply
Units

±80v d.c.
Telegraph
Signalling
Supply

110 v d.c.
Motor
Supply

Tunny Rack   As remembered by Gil Hayward, Frank Crofts and Ken Halton

Ken Halton
15-1-94

It may well have been Sir Herbert's involvement with the cattle that possibly laid the foundation – no pun intended – for the actual siting of the very first computer, for when 'F' block and its annexe was built in early 1943, the ha-ha ditch saved a lot of earth moving for the footings of the annexe. And the annexe was where the first Colossus was destined to stand. The main frame was positioned about 15 yards in from where the line of York stones can be seen.

'F' block and its annexe were separated by the small road which virtually bisects the whole of the Park at this point. Joining the two buildings was an archway or bridge somewhat similar to that found in the stable block. 'F' block was one of the largest buildings erected during this phase of building on the Park and was built to similar standards as the bombe unit, but on a much bigger scale. The central corridor alone was 25 feet wide and later, when space was once more at a premium, an additional row of offices was actually built in the corridor itself. The block can rightly claim to have housed some of the most important machines developed during the war and as such these were housed, like the bombes, behind considerable layers of steel and concrete. The annexe followed the same construction pattern.

In the southern wings of 'F' block Hitler's personal messages were decoded by some of these machines. The German codes being used were given the embracing name 'Fish' by Bletchley and included individual codes such as Jellyfish, Tunny, etc. The 'F' block work was yet another expansion area, this time from the original team set up by Major Ralph Tester in 'B' block. Known therefore as 'the Testery', codes handled here included the Tunny which was the product of the German Lorenz machine and not the Geheimschreiber, as is often incorrectly stated. The Lorenz was a semi-automatic, multi-rotor machine, and as such a great advance on the basic three rotor Enigma and the improved four rotor machine. Once cryptographers had found the wheel settings of the Lorenz, these were passed to the Tunny machine operators who set up their machines in an emulation exercise. Then the intercepted encyphered tape was fed into Tunny and, if Bletchley was lucky, out came plain German text. In finding the wheel settings, cryptographers used Colossus.

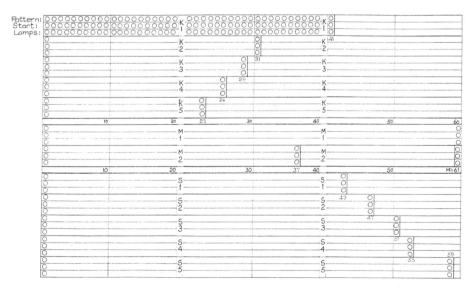

All jacks used for K1 are shown; 1, 60 and 61 are shown for M1 and first and last for other wheels.

Tunny ~ Jack Field   As remembered by Gil Hayward and Ken Halton

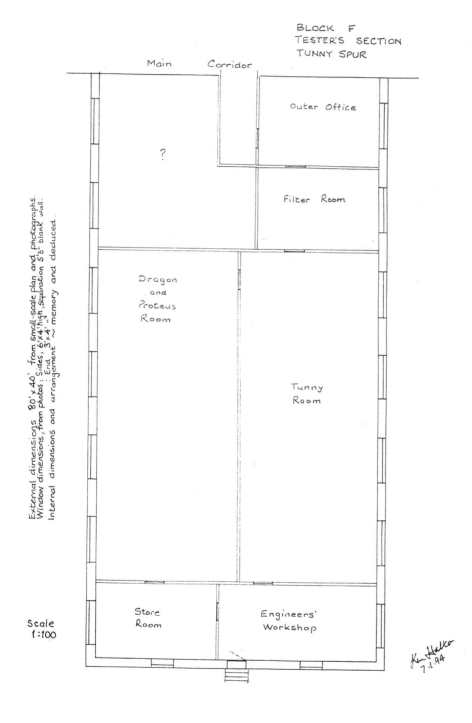

BLOCK F
TESTER'S SECTION
TUNNY SPUR

Main   Corridor

Outer Office

?

Filter Room

Dragon
and
Proteus
Room

Tunny
Room

External dimensions 80'x40' from small-scale plan and photographs.
Window dimensions, from photos: Sides, 6'x4' high, separation 5'3" blank wall.
Internal dimensions and arrangement ~ memory and deduced.

Store
Room

Engineers'
Workshop

Scale
1:100

Ken Hallco
7.1.94

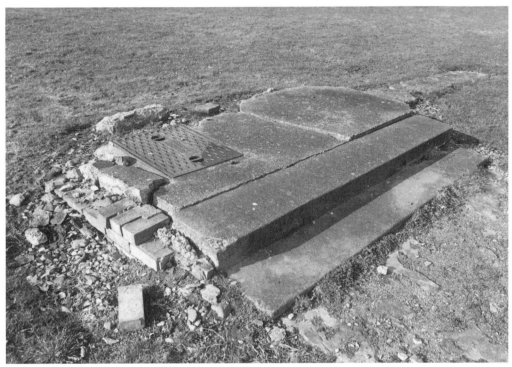

The step into the annexe building, never removed by the demolition contractor, with part of the foundations.

In the northern four wings of 'F' block Japanese codes were being decyphered. These four wings, the last wartime building to be carried out in the Park, were added in the spring of 1944 and fed from services coming out of the smaller 'G' block, some 50 yards away and closest of all the buildings to the wooded copse that still remains. All of the Axis powers involved in the war were having codes broken by personnel in 'F' block which, in total, housed five Colossus computers. These computers proved invaluable to the Allies in respect of the speed and grades of codes they could break, along with the quality of information that they yielded. Some of this work is still classified so we may never know the full story of 'F' block's wartime role.

In 1987 British Telecom, whether in ignorance or acting under orders, we shall never know, demolished both block and annexe. The story goes that the company called in a contractor who surveyed the buildings from outside and said he could have the lot down in three weeks. Well, it was only bricks and mortar, wasn't it? The allotted time span came and went and he was still trying to get the window frames out of the annexe. The Trust has a video recording of the attempts to demolish the main block and the steel ball swinging from its hawser and crane merely bounces along the roof like a table-tennis ball. Eventually it did all come down – after the jibs of at least two cranes were bent in the exercise – all that is except for one corner footing of the annexe and its main steps. They are there for the world to see, all that remains of buildings that were home to machines which have changed the course of history and now are such an integral part of our everyday life.

Numbers one and two of the ten Colossus machines were housed in the annexe and with the five in the main block, this accounts for seven

'H' Block, *the heavily reinforced homes of further Colossus machines. The grassed area in front is the northern edge of the annexe site.*

of the ten in use. The other three, numbers three, four and five, were accommodated in 'H' block, which still stands, to the north, or behind, the annexe site when viewed from the position of the ha-ha wall. These three machines were installed around the summer of 1944, during the early days of the Normandy operations, and they played a major role in the intelligence process surrounding the invasion of mainland Europe.

8. 'D' Block and 'G' Block

All of the brick and concrete blocks built on the Park made up the second phase of building and this was completed in an extremely short space of time. 'A' and 'B' blocks, which are reviewed later, were built in late 1941 and early 1942, followed by the rest in a flurry of activity over the next two years.

'D' block, which still stands to the south-east of the 'F' block grassed area, gives an indication of how the now demolished 'F' block might have looked. The next stop on the tour, it is again very heavily constructed, with the typical wide central corridor and a series of spurs, or wings, some thirteen in all, running from this. The building was completed in May 1943, about the same time as Bletchley's British personnel were reinforced by a contingent of American staff. Its main entrance has a fort-like quality about it and what is now the front car park was, during the latter war years, a very large mound of earth to give additional bomb-blast protection.

The building was broken into three areas with the ever-expanding Hut 3, with its priority and analysis tasks, acquiring the western wings. These wings were to handle all the intelligence planning, monitoring of information gathering and decoding for the Normandy invasion. One particular instance gives a clear insight into one area of opportunity. On 4 and 5 May 1944 the Japanese Ambassador in Berlin inspected the German defences built to counter the invasion threat and known as the Atlantic Wall. Normally the Japanese Embassy used what were called 'hand cyphers' but on this occasion the Ambassador chose to send his report to Tokyo by way of an Enigma transmission. His report, duly picked up and then decoded at Bletchley, stated that: 'Although the defensive sea wall and its support is very good, the morale of the troops manning the wall is very low.' Winston Churchill personally marked the decrypt as 'important' and there is reason to believe that General Eisenhower

'D' block in the background – more than 65,000 square feet of working space. The modern roundabout in the foreground replaced the massive wartime open-topped water tank, kept filled for water supplies in case of fire.

One of the Hut 3 priority teams hard at work in Bletchley Park with civilian and service personnel working together.

took the information into strong account when deciding on the June landing date.

As the workload of Hut 3 necessitated the expansion of premises, a similar situation was existing with the other old wooden huts. Hut 6 needed more space for its army and Luftwaffe sections, as did the naval sections operating from Huts 4 and 8. Both then took over large areas in 'D' block, Hut 6 moving into another four wings of the building.

The work accomplished here, in respect of breaking newer and more advanced German codes as well as ten new Enigma keys, proved vitally important. As Sir Harry Hinsley wrote in volume three, part two, of *British Intelligence in the Second World War*, by the spring of 1944 'most of the keys and their associated frequencies and call-signs had been identified'. It was part of the overall task which was to give the Allies mastery of the skies over France, so much so that German infantry had a saying at the time: 'If the planes overhead are silver, they are American; if they are camouflaged, they are British; and if they are not there at all, they are German!' Alongside all of this, the section still found time to use part of the building to train new staff.

The naval sections expanded into another two wings where the dour second Battle of the Atlantic continued to be fought, its ultimate victory being yet another ingredient vital to the strategic planning for D-Day, 6 June 1944. Though everything being done by anybody at Bletchley at that time was history in the making, the naval section managed to steal the march in one particular aspect.

Earlier, mention was made of radio Station X being disbanded in Bletchley Park and relocated to Whaddon Hall for fear of its signals being tracked down. From then, until the late spring of 1944, no direct radio communication operated from the Park. Naval intelligence, although at this time fully appreciating the speed with

The fort-like entrance to 'D' block, its windows now boarded. During the war the pictured car park was a huge mound of earth, piled there as blast protection.

'D' block, from the mound on its side nearest the railway, showing its massive permanence even more clearly. The corner of 'G' block is on the right.

which Bletchley could crack a coded message and relay its contents to commanders in the field (something like thirty minutes was not unheard of), suggested that additional precious time could be saved if, for the D-Day landings, radio messages could be received directly in the Park.

The request apparently went to the highest authority, Churchill himself, and after a great deal of deliberation was granted. Temporary aerials immediately sprouted skyward at the rear of 'D' block, close to the wooded area, and were used for a few short weeks immediately before and after the Normandy landings. The difference it made to naval operations within Operation Overlord, the code name for D-Day, was significant and justified the Navy argument. Against this background can be seen not only how important was the Navy's contribution to the land invasion, but also what high priority was being placed on Bletchley's overall role by Government.

Since the Bletchley Park Trust has unpicked more and more of the 'D' block role in the Normandy landings, former personnel have said that they 'worked underground'. They are unable to remember exact locations and stories of underground bunkers do abound. But there is now a substantial amount of evidence to suggest that such a command complex did exist, and its location was of importance to the workings of 'D' block. Both the Trust and British Telecom, who have given a great deal of assistance in this area, have carried out digs and probes to try and ascertain whether such a command complex did exist. But to date, I regret, there is nothing to report.

One wing of 'D' block is different to all the others. It is much smaller and has no access other than entrance through the main block's front door, unlike other wings which do have minor entrances. Security here was an obvious priority. This wing was used as the administration wing and houses a 'strong room'. In January 1944, four meetings were held in the wing by the heads of the Intelligence Services and the operational heads of Overlord. Those attending these meetings discussed the intelligence requirements of the overall battle plan and were briefed with maps of the Normandy beaches and sand tray models. During the next three months more meetings drew in more specialists, including Americans from 21st Army group, the main group dealing with the land battle.

It is not unrealistic to suppose that many of the Overlord plans and charts were locked up for safe keeping in the strong room, and we can now see just how important was Bletchley Park's role in the launching of the 'second front' in 1944.

An exterior door to one of the 'D' block wings showing its blast-proof wall.

'G' block from the mound. The concrete block with its steel hook protruding may have been the base of one of the straining wires holding the temporary aerials used either side of D-Day, 6 June 1944.

Once the invasion began, GC&CS expected to deal with 2,000 priority decrypts a day; as events were to unfold, Bletchley dealt with some 4,840 signals a day for several weeks following the landings. Broken down, about 2,000 of these were naval decrypts and about 2,500 army and air force decrypts. And, it must be remembered, this was Bletchley's effort in only one of several theatres of war.

To the immediate north of 'D' block is 'G' block which was built as a follow-on programme. During the war it was physically linked to 'D' but in later years a brick partition was built to make the two buildings independent. Many of the departments operating on the wartime Park were housed in 'G' block in 1944 and 1945 and it also became the training building for detachments of American and Canadian staff who were to operate the Special Liaison Units that

Field Marshal Montgomery, pictured on the Normandy beaches following the Allied landings of 1944. The campaign was to bring more arguments with Prime Minister Churchill over strategy and tactics.

worked directly with Bletchley Park in the field. As this was built later on in the war years it is not so heavily constructed as 'D' and 'F' and is also a two storey building, echoing the earliest concrete, brick and steel buildings in the Park, 'A' and 'B' block, of which more later.

9. The Card Index

At the bottom end of 'D' block, that is the wing of the building nearest the railway station, the dissecting road swings almost due south so that eventually it leads into a full loop to return to the Mansion. On this corner is a small, single storey, heavily constructed block that in the war years housed the library of information gathered from all sections

'Debs Delight', the oft-forgotten 'C' block which housed the card index system. The greenhouse type structures on the roof were added after the war to admit more light. Again, a heavily constructed building.

operating in Bletchley Park and beyond. Stored on white, 5 by 4 inch filing cards, every conceivable scrap of intelligence was catalogued, whether it was from direct decrypts or snippets picked up in 'plain language' by the 'Y' station operators.

The cards were stored in thousands of brown cardboard boxes and each card was individually photographed at specific intervals. The photographs were then sent to the Bodleian Library in Oxford in case back-up retrieval was ever needed. Reports also indicate that a third set may have been sent to a location near Manchester, but this is not substantiated.

Many of the staff were civilian females, a proportion of whom it seems may have come from upper class families, for 'C' block was given the nickname 'Debs Delight'. The tale is that, unqualified for any of the women's service arms but determined to 'do their bit', the debutantes were drafted to Bletchley Park as filing clerks. Though this was not perhaps what the family had in mind, the compensation was that the work was highly secret and therefore the nature of the day to day task was never revealed.

With hindsight, Debs Delight can now be seen as something of a cruel jibe. For both rich or poor families, war work was a great leveller and the card index rooms in 'C' block were just as important to the overall GC&CS structure as anything else. The clerks did a magnificent job.

Some of what was considered to be lower grade intelligence, but still stored on the cards, was able to contribute directly to field matters on occasion. There is one story that 'Y' station operatives, skilled in listening to morse signals coming over the air, were able to pinpoint the individual German signallers 'touch' and in due course obtained personal details of such signallers – name, rank, unit, interests, etc. One signaller, operating from within France on a certain frequency, suddenly 'dried up', and the 'Y' service operators wondered what had happened to him. A short time later his 'touch' was recognized coming from a completely different location, and so this was reported to Bletchley. It was logged on card index and duly reported, and by this means Allied commanders knew that a particular German unit had moved its headquarters.

At one stage the card index unit was visited by a high ranking American officer who was amazed at the orderly rows of brown cardboard boxes. His words, with some licence, were along the lines of: 'Goddamn, if this were the Pentagon, there would be rows and rows of shiny filing cabinets with nothing in them, and you do it all in Goddamn shoe boxes!' British resourcefulness was recognized even then, it seems. Later, by a quirk of fate, the educational aspects of card-indexing were to reappear when, after the war, the building was made into classrooms for technical training.

10. Safe Against Gas

I must beg the reader's indulgence here in reminding that our tour does not follow building on the Park in chronological order but follows more the site's geography. For this reason, when the visitor turns away from 'Debs Delight', the card index block, and moves back toward the Mansion via the road skirting the lake, the blocks now on view, and the last to be visited between these covers, were the earliest put up in phase two of construction, being erected in late 1941 and early 1942.

The inner parkland gardens of 'A' and 'B' block, now the favourite haunt of rabbits and squirrels.

Like the other brick and concrete blocks, these buildings, 'A', 'B', and 'E' blocks, are also heavily constructed and are reinforced with more than 200 bracing steel girders. Following Germany's abortive attempt at invasion in 1940, the fear of gas attack by the Luftwaffe was still very real and 'A' block, particularly, was given certain protective measures. These included hermetically sealing doors and heavy window blinds, features not found anywhere else in the Park's extensive building programme.

The block has no central corridor as have the other major buildings, so it had no large wings. Instead, it has small stubs, or spurs, four in all, the first being smaller than the other three. In this first stub, nearest to naval wooden Hut 8, were some of the Park's early teleprinters, installed by GPO engineers. The second stub was the first expansion of the naval sections, operating from Huts 4 and 8, and on the ground floor one of the major visual features of the working offices was the very large wall charts of the Atlantic. The positions and movements of

The lower half of 'B' block adjacent to the card index block. It was on the top floor here that Capt. Roy Jenkins worked on the 'Fish' codes.

'A' and 'B' pictured in winter sunshine from across the lake. But the ever present bike shed cannot be denied!

German U-boats were carefully plotted on the charts as information came in.

Before reaching 'A' block, however, the visitor passes 'B' block and its rooms or offices known as the Testery, after its team leader Major Ralph Tester, at the time of writing now aged over ninety and living in Oxford. Testery work, it will be recalled, also went on later in 'F' block. Academics, among them a young Army captain named Roy Jenkins and now Lord Jenkins of parliamentary fame, toiled away here at breaking the codes from the Lorenz machine, dealt with in Chapter 7.

Behind 'A' and 'B', but opposite 'D' block and fronting the dividing site road, is 'E' block. Like all other later buildings 'E' saw a variety of team tasks as the overall workload expanded, including decyphering messages, with service personnel and civilians working side by side. Many of the cypher clerks were Foreign Office staff who, at the outbreak of war, were posted to Bletchley without the faintest idea of what to expect. On arrival, they went through the normal procedures relating to the Official Secrets Act and then reported to Elmers School, close to St Mary's church, for intensive training. The whole operation was very 'hush-hush', to use the language of the day.

At Elmers each phase of their training was closely monitored and they had to pass in each phase before moving on. Only when it was deemed that they could operate a cypher machine were they then allowed to enter the Park. Here they were allocated to a team operating in a particular block where the work was arduous and often lonely, despite the rapid growth of personnel on site until it reached its maximum of some seven thousand. Friendships were struck up with team members, but it was not considered right to become too friendly with people outside your own immediate working environment. As one lady doing this job in 'E' block has written to tell the Trust: 'You could hardly go up to anyone and say "Hello, what do you do?", it was forbidden.' So, too, was the use of cameras so there are very few snapshots today of day to day life on the Park. However, there is a happy ending to this particular tale. At the end of the war the lady in question was moved to another block when 'E' closed down and found herself in the company of a young man who was one of the team that built Colossus. Later they married and had two sons and five grandchildren. Long after the war other husbands and wives discovered that they had both worked at the Park in the 1940s but, secrecy being as it was, neither had mentioned it to the other.

The pattern of work was a week of days, a week of evenings and a week of nights, and nobody liked the nights. To lighten the load, especially in quieter moments – which were not that often – a gramophone would be cranked up and music would filter through the block. A particular favourite of 'E' block was Bing Crosby and the Andrews Sisters with their rendering of 'Don't fence me in'. Appropriate, perhaps, for staff on the Park, but played almost to destruction.

With 'A' and 'B' enjoying a prime position in the Park fronting the lake, it is not difficult to see why, in 1949, the Civil Aviation Authority took these buildings and 'E' block for its training school with residential accommodation. Of all the wartime buildings on the Park these have been kept in excellent repair and show how good they can look, fifty years on, given the right treatment. The lake, of course, is appealing at any time of the year and its ducks and geese have given scores of

Jemima and friends on the Park's frozen lake in November 1993. But where she is now remains yet another of the Park's secrets.

Bletchley children for decades the opportunity to dispose of their stale bread and broken biscuits.

The water has its resident heron, who dines well on the teeming goldfish beneath the surface, but pride of place as number one character must go to Jemima, the only white duck, who met visitors far from the water's edge to make sure she was the first to be fed. Just before Christmas 1993, though, she disappeared. Did a fox make a meal of her, or is this to be another Park secret never to be revealed? Perhaps someone knows what happened to her.

But now the brief tour is completed and the visitor is back where Britain's best kept secret began, at the Mansion.

11. The Bletchley Park Trust

The Bletchley Park Trust came into being on 13 February 1992, three days after Milton Keynes Borough Council declared most of Bletchley Park a conservation area. It was a fitting beginning, perhaps, in what was to be a long and arduous campaign to gain recognition of the Park as a heritage site and to save it for the nation.

The steering committee had moved quickly since its first meeting some four months earlier. Roger Bristow was engaged as a general manager, Tony Sale was a one-day-a-week consultant and between them they had produced for the committee a business plan, the main thrust of which remains Trust policy to this day. What the plan outlined was the setting up on site of a series of high-tech museums, the first two of which would be museums to the work of the wartime cryptographers and to the history of the computer. National museums dedicated to telecommunications, to mark the old Post Office role on the site and BT's later ownership, and to radar and air traffic control, to mark the secret work undertaken on radar in the 1940s and the setting up of the Civil Aviation Authority's telecommunication engineers training establishment from 1949 onwards, would follow.

The core of this plan, and its subsequent amendments to date, was that the museums would be as self-sufficient as possible so that there would be little or no drain on the public purse. This might at first seem an impossible objective, for it is a well-known fact of museum life that few, if any, make a profit or even break even. The difference with the Bletchley Park museums was that they would employ a business framework pioneered within the new city of Milton Keynes, of which Bletchley is now an integral part. That framework is now widely known in the voluntary sectors of social, environmental and arts provision as the Milton Keynes balancing package.

Prior to the building of Milton Keynes social provision tended to come after initial development and was totally funded from the public purse – libraries, swimming baths, community halls and the like. Milton Keynes set about changing that social infrastructure by ensuring that the building of, say, community meeting places, was part of the initial contract to a builder who had won the order to develop a particular housing area. Within the same contract, or another running alongside, the developer would build the housing area's shopping provision. When the whole was complete, rents from the shops would provide staffing and running costs for the community meeting place. The one balanced out the other and there was no drain on the public purse. With the Trust's business plan for the Park, key buildings will be used for museum provision while other buildings, duly refurbished, can be leased out, so providing income.

The steering committee approached a dozen or more people, who had expressed an interest in the plan, to become Trustees. Professor Peter Thewlis, head of the then Milton Keynes Polytechnic, now the De Montfort University, was elected chairman, and Sir Philip Duncombe, vice-chairman. The Trust was duly registered as a charity and, with permission from the Civil Aviation Authority, began to hold regular meetings in its buildings – the old 'A' block – on the Park. The Trust's offices, from which Roger Bristow and his wife Ruth so ably operated, were about a mile away at Denbigh.

The workload grew as the office drew up a strategy to persuade Government and BT to give the Trust single tender status when they, as owners, were ready to dispose of the Park. By this time early retirement had beckoned me with the wind-up of the Milton Keynes Development Corporation, its task of planning the new city and overseeing much of its actual building deemed complete by the Department of the Environment. This was, of course, the same Government department that owned Bletchley Park and whom we were trying to persuade to grant the Trust single tender status. The Department's answer to this was a firm 'no' and came about the same time as I said 'yes' to taking the paid, four days a week post of Trust chief executive. So much for an early retirement!

The next year seemed to fly past in a flurry of political activity and fund raising on as many fronts and in as many ways as was possible. Tony, Roger and I, labelled 'the Grand Triumvirate' after particular golfing champions of sixty or more years earlier, were joined in our ranks as full and part-time staff by Warrant Officer Ray Dawson, RAOC, retiring after twenty-five years service. It was Ray who set up

'The Grand Triumvirate' on site. Left to right: Roger Bristow, Ted Enever and Tony Sale.

the Queensway, Bletchley, Trust shop when we acquired the premises on most favourable terms and who handled much of the administration in the early days of our 'Friends of Bletchley Park' scheme. In January 1993 we were able to move the Trust office from Denbigh to rooms above the shop where, as always, Ruth organized us with quiet efficiency.

The Triumvirate, by now sometimes called Foggy, Compo and Clegg after the 'Summer Wine' characters, or even something totally unprintable if someone thought we hadn't got it right, beavered away at trying to break down the bureaucratic doors of Government's Property Holdings, the organization responsible for the Park's ultimate disposal, and the property managers of BT. We seemed to go to endless meetings either at the Mansion or in London offices, and produce endless variations of the business plan, but to no avail. In desperation, it was decided to write direct to the Secretary of State for the Environment, Michael Howard, who we knew was aware of our project following the initial October '91 letter to Prime Minister John Major and with whom we had already consulted.

It was one of those moves that can perhaps be best described as a flash of inspiration coupled with sheer, blind panic, for it did the trick. The Minister wrote back to say that he was fully supportive of our aims, and that he would do what he could to help. The Trust had always said it would pay a fair price for the Park, though a lease would be preferable, and so we then entered into a phase of meetings on land values and planning constraints now that the Park was mostly a conservation area.

Throughout all of this, and mostly unbeknown to the Trust, the Borough Council was taking due note and our support from its elected members and officers was growing daily.

Internally, changes were underway. With funds ever a headache, as with any charity, it was reluctantly decided, in March 1993, that the consultancies paid to Tony, Ray and myself would need to be curtailed. Roger would stay on as anchor man in the office with Ruth. Ray, to his credit, bit the bullet and continued to run the shop for free. Tony came over whenever he could and became a Trustee, as did I, the pair of us now eligible as we were not paid advisors. Roger's new role merged into some of my former tasks as chief executive while I tended to concentrate on the marketing and promotional aspects of the project on a now purely voluntary basis.

The main negotiations with the owners were taken over by the chairman and a small group of Trustees but again it was to Michael

A revival of the Bletchley Park show in June 1993 brought this collection of Second World War vehicles parked outside the Mansion. The Military Vehicles Trust now has trucks and lorries permanently housed in the Park; they go on display at open weekends and are driven around the grounds.

Howard that we were indebted for the next quantum leap. Invited by Mike Bett, the vice-chairman of BT, to view the site, the Trust was asked to give the Minister and Mr Bett a presentation of its aims and objectives when that visit took place, in May 1993. The presentation went ahead at the De Montfort University.

It was clear at this presentation that both men were impressed with the range and detail of the project, its visual clarity much enhanced by the professional skills of architect David Hartley, who had offered his help to the Trust a year or more earlier. To our surprise, Mr Bett invited us all to accompany him and the Minister to the Park, where David Hartley showed the Minister the key buildings and gave a brief history of their work at what seemed breakneck speed. At the end of the visit, the Minister paid the Trust a glowing compliment. 'You have achieved a great deal with very limited resources,' he said, 'but it is now clear you need some extra help. I am going away to get you that help.'

The Minister was true to his word. Within a very short space of time a proposal was put to the Trust which suggested that an independent feasibility study be carried out into our aims and objectives, the major task being to ensure that our business plan was viable. The Trust was to

Dear Prime Minister,

You will recall from previous correspondence that a year ago today, 19 October, some 140 codebreakers who served at Bletchley Park, Milton Keynes, charged the local community to save the site from demolition.

Accordingly the Bletchley Park Trust was formed and the petition before you is from the Trust calling on Government to donate its holdings in the Park to the nation. The petition has attracted world-wide support, particularly from our European and American friends, and I would ask you to give the matter your most serious consideration.

The Trust plans to establish within the Park a campus of high-tech museums to commemorate the role of the Park during the second world war. However, I would stress that the project in no way seeks to glorify war or gloat in victory all these years on. The Trust views the campus as a monument to man's intellect and seeks to encourage education and training facilities on site so that younger generations, in particular, not only in this country but internationally, can learn and benefit from our country's heritage.

This, of course, is not the first time Bletchley Park has sought direct help from Downing Street. Fifty one years ago at this time, codebreakers wrote to Winston Churchill for additional resources. These were granted immediately and delivering the petition today is one of those original signatories, Sir Stuart Milner-Barry. Sir Michael Alexander, the son of another signatory, Hugh Alexander, is also in the petition party.

The letter to Prime Minister John Major accompanying a 10,000 signature petition. Government is now backing the Trust's plans.

be an equal partner alongside BT and Government in selecting the consultants to carry out the work, but the costs of the study would be shared jointly between the owners. We could not really have asked for more – it was fair on all three parties.

Consultants were duly invited to tender, short-listed and the Trust chairman had a seat on the final selection panel. The task went to Coopers and Lybrand who began their work in the late summer of 1993. While this was taking place, but in a separate arena, the local government planning inspectorate were reassessing the development plan for Bletchley after having taken evidence from the Trust and agents for the owners. The latter were still pressing for residential development on those parts of Bletchley Park not covered by the Borough Council's conservation

The Trust party outside No. 10 Downing Street with the petition. Left to right: Ted Enever, Sir Stuart Milner-Barrie, Sir Michael Alexander, Tony Sale and Professor David Lock, planning advisor to the Trust.

order, which itself had been extended to encompass all the wartime buildings on site as its full historical implications became better known. The inspectorate's final deliberations made it clear that the historic detail uncovered by the Trust since 1991 made the site one of great value to the nation's heritage and therefore the Borough Council, as the local planning authority, must take this into account when dealing with any residential planning applications for the site. The report was enough to persuade the owners to withdraw all their planning applications.

Meantime, Michael Howard had gone to the Home Office following a Cabinet reshuffle, his place at the DoE being taken by John Gummer. Like his predecessor, he was to prove most supportive.

The Coopers and Lybrand study was completed by the late summer and upheld the Trust's argument over the previous two years that the

Milton Keynes mayor, Cllr Les Hostler, is greeted by Trust chairman Professor Peter Thewlis at the Trust's first open day in February 1994. Providing the suitable wartime look is Roger Beningfield, of Leighton Buzzard, the owner of the Humber staff car. The car was that used by General Horrocks.

On the weekend of the D-Day anniversary, Tony Sale explains the workings of the Enigma machine at the Trust's exhibition in the Park. Note the boxed spare sets of rotor wheels.

scheme was viable if run on balancing package lines. It proposed a modest start to the ultimate museum complex, or campus as it was more usually being called, and all three parties agreed to accept the study's findings as the way forward. It was now a question of waiting to see what sort of deal the owners would offer the Trust, but to all intents and purposes, we had achieved what we had set out to do. The Park and its wartime buildings were saved.

Meetings with Government were soon under way and the Trust was given permission to begin clearing and refurbishing buildings in the Park ready for its first phase of development. Leases would be granted in due course. Nothing was heard from BT, but the Trust felt able to go ahead with its scheme.

Trust offices were opened in the Park in December 1993 and by February 1994 the site was opened on alternate weekends to a receptive

Veterans of the Combined Services Associations parade from the Park to St Mary's, Bletchley parish church, for a D-Day commemorative service on Sunday 5 June. The Park hosted two days of events to mark the 50th anniversary of the Normandy landings.

Martin Baggott, right, is interviewed in Bletchley Park by a BBC Three Counties radio reporter on the recovery of a crashed wartime Mosquito aircraft at nearby Wavendon. With his colleagues of the Buckinghamshire Aircraft Recovery group, also pictured, they have mounted their own exhibition on site as part of the Trust's overall and varied attractions.

paying public. A basic exhibition has now grown and other exhibitions, including one of Churchill memorabilia, were ready for the D-Day 50th anniversary commemorations in June. In these early days I would ask the public to enjoy what they see, but to look beyond that to our plans for the future. Bletchley Park will not be rooted in the past, though it is important that we recognize this heritage. But, like the Park of 1940, it will also be innovative and progressive, and its museums, I am sure, will offer the public the chance to see, at first hand, the forefront of modern technology in a whole range of disciplines.

It has been an extremely arduous campaign, taking much time and energy and producing frustrations and annoyances along the way. But the Trust's small voice has been heard and recognized, the hallmark of a democracy which those early codebreakers fought to keep alive fifty and more years ago. Though Bletchley Park in those war years will always be known as Britain's best kept secret, the Park now has a viable and exciting future, a future in which the nation as a whole can share and take part.